INVEST IN YOURSELF

BEING YOUR OWN BANK

PERI SCOTT

BYOB
Be Your Own Bank

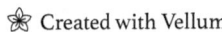

For my Family
Because of you, I am a rich man.

DISCLAIMER

I am just a regular guy. I came up with these ideas from experimentation and modifying ideas from other disciplines. I am not a financial planner or an accountant or any other type of financial professional. Do not take what I suggest as financial advice. They are just ideas.

PREFACE

The best part of coming up with a great idea, for me, is getting to share it with others. I love to watch the expressions on peoples' faces as they start to understand what I am talking about and the wheels begin to turn. The excitement they start to feel when they realize that what I am saying makes sense is contagious, and I feel it again like it's the first time, every time.

That feeling has been happening a lot lately as I hear from readers of my first book BYOB - Be Your Own Bank. I am constantly being bombarded with questions asking me to clarify, expand and suggest modifications of the ideas I put forth in that book. People are excited and eager to get started with the program as they see that there is actually a practical way to create a family fortune starting with what you have right now.

I am so grateful and proud that the book has helped people. It has opened their eyes to a new way of looking at finance, wealth, investing and leverage. I never expected such an enthusiastic reception to its ideas.

That being said, I also realized that there are a lot of

people who are starting out at a bit of a disadvantage. It was sobering to observe how many people have very little, to zero information at all about how money works. They only know what their parents had taught them, or what they stumbled upon in their own everyday life. They believed all kinds of myths and misconceptions about how to manage and invest money. They were never given a financial education of any kind and the ideas in my book seemed magical to them because they never knew those things were even possible.

With that in mind, I decided to make the goal if this book to go a little deeper into the details of some of the mechanisms I discuss in my first book, clarify a few ideas, and offer some modified strategies that might help simplify the path to financial freedom. My hope is that I can offer some guidance to everyone who desires financial freedom, no matter where they are starting from.

Although reading the first book will create context for the ideas in this one, I will attempt to make this book stand on its own. I hope you find value in its pages and hope in its message.

Peri Scott June, 2019

INTRODUCTION

Financial Freedom is attainable. It is not reserved for the privileged or the already wealthy. It is attainable for almost everyone who lives in a free society and has the ability to earn money. It is not super hard, but it required discipline, which *is* super hard. You just haven't been taught how. You haven't learned the principles by which money is grown.

I love the line in the movie "Good Will Hunting" (spoiler alert) where therapist Dr. Sean Maguire (Robin Williams) says to the hero, Will Hunting (Matt Damon),

"It's not your fault"

It is a powerful scene, and is a pivotal moment in the story. Upon realizing that, "It isn't his fault" he finally accepts responsibility for his own life and awakens to the fact that he is not a victim of his past, but the master of his future.

Having presented my wealth building strategies to the general public in my first book, **BYOB - Be Your Own Bank**, I learned a great many things from readers' feedback. Two stood out:

1. My ideas were appreciated
2. Most people knew very little about money

I was thrilled that people loved my ideas and were using them to pursue financial freedom, but I was taken aback by the lack of knowledge about "financial matters" that existed. At first I thought,

"How can people be so apathetic?"

Then I realized that,

"It's not your fault"

People just haven't been taught these things. And worst of all, didn't realize that they needed to know!

The importance of financial education is more important than ever these days as inflation is out of control, jobs are no longer safe and pensions are a thing of the past. People need to take control of their own financial destiny, not give it over to some "expert" that has no incentive to make decisions that benefit anyone but the corporate shareholders.

People need to take matters into their own hands and educate themselves. They need to learn how money works, how leverage works, how investing works and how to maximize their own efforts at becoming financially free. It is especially dangerous to just ignore it, or hope that things will work out eventually. The world is a bit too harsh for that approach, I'm afraid.

Financially Free means different things to different people and that is okay. What is important is that you have the goal in mind. I love the new F. I. R. E. movement (Financial Independence Retire Early) because it really is a sign of the times. People are waking up to the realization that they don't have to spend 40 years in a cubicle until they can do what they want. They are blogging about it, writing books about it, talking about it on YouTube and *actually* doing it. The goal being - **Financial Freedom**, in whatever form that takes for you. People are aspiring to "retire" early, sometimes in their 20's, to travel the world, start new fulfilling careers or just discover themselves. They are learning how to live frugally, more from a standpoint of prioritizing what is really important, than from pure stoicism. They are learning how to live off of much less than their income and invest the rest. They are blogging about how to hack the system and exploring ways to pursue their dreams without going the traditional route of working 9 to 5.

This paradigm tends to be more prevalent with the younger generation and I can see why. Millennials tend to think about deeper things than older people do and ask questions that shake up the old rules. I love that they question the futility of working for other people and challenge the "be a good employee" mindset. They care about the planet, human rights, and they search for meaning. A lot of older people find this attitude flaky and irresponsible, but I personally, love it. I believe that we really NEED to think outside the box to truly change the world. I also believe changing the world starts with changing yourself.

I want to challenge your beliefs here. I want you to think outside of the box. The traditional box that says, "Do as you're told" and "Give me your money to invest". You are going to be given a few ideas and some tools that you can use to take back control of your future. You will learn how to make financial decisions that maybe seem a little rash. That is the point. I want you to be a little uncomfortable. These ideas are a little unconventional but I hope that they are an effective way to get you to *truly believe* that your idea of financial freedom is actually possible. I want you to know that you can have anything you dream of, if you have the right tools and information.

I am going to get you to think a little bit more like an entrepreneur. Maybe not a traditional business owner, who is a slave to his business and doesn't take a vacation for twelve years, but the new kind of entrepreneur that creates a passive income producing empire that runs itself. I want you to see that there are different ways of doing things.

In my first book, BYOB, I suggested that the rich do things differently when it comes to money and offered a method to grow and keep your wealth. I am still convinced that they have it right. The great thing is, you don't have to be rich to manage wealth in the exact same way. What matters is the principles, not the amounts. In this book, I offer you some additional strategies and some refinements that will continue that quest. You can enjoy the same mathematically proven benefits that the ultra wealthy do, just by learning the principles, philosophy, and mechanisms that grow your wealth automatically.

You are free to use each piece as a stand-alone tool, or combine them into a money flowing machine. It is up to you. My goal is to get you to learn and appreciate that these new ways of implementing money management are legitimate options that your mom and dad maybe didn't know. If they did, you might not be reading this book.

I want you to come away with a new perspective on what is considered "safe" and "practical" when it comes to your financial future. What worked in the past isn't necessarily going to always be the way it is. The only thing you can count on to be persistent is change. And the rate of change is accelerating. Don't get left behind.

The world is not perfect and capitalism is no exception.

The question you have to ask yourself is "What CAN I Do?" to succeed in this system.

This is one of my favourite mantras. It gives you back the power in any situation. You are never a victim if you always ask yourself that question. This applies to the changing world of capitalism. You need to prepare yourself for unforeseen changes and disasters. You need to set yourself up to navigate the storms that are an inherent part of any economy. By asking yourself, "What CAN I do?", you are taking responsibility for your future.

The best way to prepare yourself for economic uncertainty is to have a plan. You need a plan that challenges the normal way of doing things. You need plan that takes care of you, not just now, but in perpetuity. True happiness means you take responsibility for everything that happens in your life, not just the good stuff. That means you try to prepare for everything. That means you get yourself a money machine that will take care of you and your family no matter what is happening in macro economics. You are going to need a system that takes you from where you are now, to where you want to be.

There are many systems out there, and I encourage you to learn about them. My system is not for everyone, but I really believe in it. I have used it myself to drive my life forward financially, and I have shared it with many people who have also used it to bring their financial lives into focus.

You can also check out my website at:

https://beyourownbank.ca

There you will find tips and advice on making the most of your money, as well as a community of like-minded people who want to learn more and share their successes.

1

VALUE

I am constantly amazed by my observation that people, generally, do not understand what it took to create society. They look at the world around them and have no clue or appreciation for what it actually took to imagine, design, plan and build it.

The roads, houses, cities, space stations and everyday products. They were all the result of years of hard work, years of planning, years of education, decades of research, centuries of scientific discovery. These facts seem lost on people. I don't get how they can be so blasé about the latest smartphone or a new innovation.

We need to remember and appreciate who's shoulders we are standing upon. The modern world is amazing, and would seem like magic to those just a century ago. We take it all for granted, yet we struggle to truly appreciate it. We live in a world of massive opportunity. We do not have to spend our time running from sabre tooth tigers, or foraging for food anymore. These occupations would have been a 24 hour a day endeavour not too long ago. Or, not too long ago, we could have been slaves and nobody would have had a problem with it. We do not realize how great we have it.

The true question is, "Are we happy?" We seem to have so much mental illness in our society. Anxiety, depression and self esteem issues. It never ends. I wonder if people who were out hunting for wild boar all day felt depressed? Did they have an existential crises every other day? I doubt it. They had purpose. As mundane as that purpose was, they had one. It was very clear, and very immediate. Kill something for food or die. That would stimulate me.

WE REQUIRE variety in our lives and in our minds. Studies show that the best antidote for anxiety and depression is, simply, variety. We need to create new neural pathways by learning, experiencing and feeling new things, ideas and information. We need to be engaged in something; something bigger than ourselves. We need to immerse ourselves in a project that is actually hard, that challenges us. We need to feel accountable to something or someone outside of ourselves.We need to grow.

I believe if we are not growing, we are dying. There is no such thing as staying the same. We don't reach adulthood at 18 and remain exactly that way for our whole lives. This simply isn't what we are about as humans. We need to change. We need challenge, pain, struggle and hardship. We need to have real world feedback following our efforts and respond accordingly. We need to reach our potential as human beings by challenging our perceived limitations. We do not need to compare ourselves to others or even to some imaginary standard set by the media. We need to be the best versions of ourselves that we can possibly be. That is the only true happiness. Pushing yourself to be the best version of you that is possible. That means stretching your comfort zone constantly. That means overcoming your insecurities and self imposed limitations. This needs to be done purely for its own sake. We need not worry or even care how it compares to anyone else. We only care about "Am I better today than I was yesterday"? It is the only thing we have control over. It is all we *should* care about. What *CAN* I do?

Movement.

Forward motion.

This is the key to happiness. Not social media likes or # of followers.

Did I learn something today? Did I gain a new skill today? Did I make someone else's life better today?

I want you to contemplate that in order to change your life, and especially your financial life, you need to change. You cannot do the same things over and over again and expect different results. You need to learn new ideas and new strategies. You also have to be willing to change your behaviours. This is difficult for most people and I am no exception.

You need to think differently. You need to understand how capitalism rewards those who produce value and tends to punish those who consume value.

You need to understand that no one is coming to rescue you. If you want financial freedom it is up to you to make the changes. It is up to you to take responsibility and it is up to you to own your results.

If the ideas I present make you a little uncomfortable, that is OK. That is part of the learning process, and it is healthy to expand your comfort zone. When it comes to money, many people have a lot of emotions attached. They tend to get upset or nervous or scared. If you want to be the master of your financial future, you need to get comfortable with money and investing. You need to learn as much as you can so it isn't as scary or uncomfortable.

This same principle applies to risk. Your risk tolerance is not a factor of who you are as a person, but is more likely a factor of how much you know. If you know what you are doing, your investing activities will be much different than if you are a beginner.

EVERYTHING WE WILL EVER ACHIEVE, gain or get in life will generally be from other people. Other people are the world. Not some sociological construct that we give life to. Every decision, every act, is from a person. We need to interact with people if we want to succeed. We need to gain people skills. We need to learn how to asses what peoples' motives are. We need to be able to understand value. The only transactions in the world that are worthwhile are win/win scenarios. We must strive for that dynamic. We will never get something for nothing. We need to provide value in exchange for value.

IN A TRADITIONAL JOB, we trade our time for money. We trade our skills to an employer in exchange for money. That money represents the benefit that the company receives, as a percentage of their revenue, that you contribute. It has nothing to do with what you "feel' you are worth. It has everything to do with the value your role brings to the company, usually in the form of "how does this add to the bottom line?". You feel you deserve a raise because you have been at the company for a long time. This means NOTHING to the business. If you are not providing more value, by contributing to the financial health of the company in a valuable way, and you can't show how your efforts directly make the company more money, then you really don't have much of a case for a raise. This is not evil corporations taking advantage of the masses. This is basic economics. Value for value. You need to find a way to deliver something that has value to someone or something else and then they will compensate you equally in wages. This is reality.

People only care what you do for them. This is a harsh truth, but it is the way it is. You value other people based on what they do for you too. Maybe they make you feel good. Maybe they feed you. Maybe they give you place to stay. Maybe they love you. It doesn't matter, it is still a value for value exchange. Value for value is the only truly healthy relationship. The value might come in the form of intangible things, but it is still there. A relationship or business transaction that is unbalanced is doomed to fail.

I mention this harsh truth in order to incentivise you to stop giving your power over to other people. They perceive your value from their perspective and I doubt it ever really matches your true value. You have a great deal to offer this world, and you should prioritize making it available. No one cares more about your success than you do. So you need to take your success into your own hands and run with it. You need to take control of your financial future and truly care for and nurture your family fortune with the utmost attention that something of that value requires. You can do it!

The investing strategies I am about to offer are tools you can use to master money. Use them in the spirit of being the best version of you, who is taking responsibility for your financial future. You are the best person to be in control of your money.

2

NEW IDEAS

I offered a few ideas and strategies in my first book, BYOB, that allow you to build a passive income producing machine from your investments. These ideas have been met with enthusiasm and many people are using them today.

As enthusiastic as my readers have been, many have asked for more information about specific parts of my strategy that I may have "glossed over". I will attempt to offer you a deeper look into some of the pieces of the "Your-Bank" plan.

In case you are new to this, my strategy involves buying dividend producing stocks and using them for the passive income they produce. I don't do stock "trading" as it is almost impossible to predict what the stock market will do (as much as some people would have you believe) and I am not a big fan of that. It is purely guessing, in my opinion, and I prefer a much more conservative approach. I like to invest based on the "yield" or dividend.

My method involves buying tried and true Blue-chip

companies that produce monthly or quarterly payouts in the form of dividends or distributions. This method allows me to receive a consistent and ever growing stream of income. My reasoning is explained more in depth in my first book, BYOB. I believe this is a great way to build wealth and create financial freedom.

The first question I always get asked is,

"What stocks should I pick"?

I refuse to answer this question as I am not a certified financial planner (nor do I play one on TV). I cannot pick stocks for you. Only you can decide which stocks you choose to purchase. As there is always risk involved in investing, it is incumbent upon you to asses that risk for yourself in the context of your own life and within the parameters that you set, based on your comfort level.

I will , however, explain my **method** for picking stocks. Good stocks come and go, but some companies have been around forever, and for good reason. They offer value. They offer things that people want . They are called "Blue-Chip Stocks". I will explain to you how I assess a good company and choose to add it to my portfolio, based on how it adds to my passive income plan.

The next question is,

"How do I decide which stock to buy more of each month"?

If you understand the principle of yield and value investing, you will make the right choice. My method is a little counter-intuitive, so I will explain more about that.

The third question,

"What is my exit strategy?"

This is a good question. I try to explain as best as I can, that there are several ways you can go, but it all depends on what your objectives are. I simply try to explain the options and mechanisms of each and let you decide.

I will also offer you a few ideas about dividend frequency and what makes for a good stock, without offering specifics.

Question #1
How to pick Stocks

WHEN CHOOSING a great stock to add to your cash flow portfolio, you are going to ignore traditional ways of stock market investing and look at a few things that apply to our philosophy:

1. Dividend Yield
2. Long Term viability
3. Distribution frequency

Dividend Yield

TRADITIONAL STOCK MARKET investors live by the mantra "buy low, sell high". That is excellent advice - *if you are psychic and can see the future.* The truth is, nobody can predict the future, and even if you are a seasoned investor who keeps track of macro-economics and interest rates and company earnings, you will probably be wrong most of the time.

Investing in the stock market hoping that your stocks will go up in price is gambling, and if you do win, it is only luck that got you there, plain and simple. Trading in index funds might give you a bit of a cushion as "in general" the whole market goes up over time, but there WILL be corrections, and unforeseen disasters that will rattle the nerves of anyone with a substantial enough stake.

In my book, BYOB, I suggest we take a slightly different approach.

We are going to evaluate the stock like a real estate investor.

When a real estate investor evaluates a commercial property like an apartment building or an office tower to add to their portfolio, they do not even care what the asking price is. They ignore the surface details and look deeper into the actual business model. They look at how much cash flow is generated by the renters each month. They then do a mathematical calculation based on earnings and expenses to come up with a value for the property. If the numbers work, they consider buying it. If they don't, they know that the seller is asking too much and grind him down or walk away. The market really doesn't dictate the price, the cash flow does.

We will pick stocks based on the cash flow too, not the market price. If the cash flow, relative to the stock price is favourable, then we consider buying it. This is called the "Yield". This is basically the return on investment or ROI that the stock has on that particular day. The yield will fluctuate from day to day, so your returns will be decided on the day you actually purchase the stock, and remain there, until you buy some more.

So if you had a portfolio of ten stocks, and some are up

and some are down, you would put your monthly contributions towards the stock that has the best yield on that day, which often times corresponds to the stock actually doing "poorly" in the stock market that day too. You are almost a contrarian investor, but there is a method to your madness.

Long Term Viability

I cannot stress enough the importance of picking stocks in great companies. By a "great company," I really mean:

1. A company that has been around for a while
2. A company that provides goods or services that are not likely to go away
3. A company that does well in good times and bad times
4. A company that has consistent dividend payouts

It is quite easy to get sucked in to a stock that is paying a really high dividend. Don't do it. Make sure the company meets all of the above criteria. Some companies take their sweet time re-adjusting their dividends during hard times, and the yield appears awesome for a while, until they reduce or eliminate it. I have seen it happen. It hurt my heart...

Do be careful not to get too carried away with the "Blue Chip" concept and invest in a company that has ben around for a hundred years, but is in a dying industry. That has also happened. My heart hurt then, too.

This might seem like a tough assignment, but it really

isn't. There are a ton of companies out there that fit the bill, and you just have to do a little research to find them. Pick companies that you believe in. Don't be greedy, and keep a cool head.

Distribution Frequency

This one is not a deal breaker by any means, but it may factor into your lifestyle preferences. If you are trying to set yourself up to live off of passive income, you may want to include some monthly distributions in your plan, vs. quarterly distributions. This is just for the sake of cash flow. Some people are really good at budgeting and having income come infrequently but I, personally, LOVE getting money every month. Call me impatient, but it makes me feel better to know that the next distribution is coming sooner, rather than later. I like to be able to know there is going to be money in my account to pay my bills, as most of my bills are monthly. This is just my preference. You need to design your system so it makes sense for you. If quarterly distributions work fine for you, great! You are living the dream! Keep going!

As you can see, I am just giving the finer details of some of the investing strategies that I talk more about in my book BYOB. To put these ideas into context, it may help to read that book first.

I will always try to make sure people understand the mechanisms of cash flow, passive income, dividends, and throw a little math at them to make sure they get the principles first. I really don't believe a paint-by-numbers approach is going to help anyone as the world changes pretty fast, and a one size fits all approach will become obsolete pretty darn quickly. If you understand the underlying principles, it is a lot easier to change your strategy and adapt to changing market conditions or policies. You need empowerment, not an instruction manual.

Question #2
Portfolio Management

As I MENTIONED, how many stocks and which ones are in your portfolio is totally up to you. For the sake of simplicity, I suggest you keep a portfolio of 10 to 12 stocks of blue-chip companies and once a month, when you make your monthly contributions, invest in the company that is performing poorly from a traditional point of view. It is likely that stock's yield is going up! You don't care about the stock price just the yield. This gives you a great ROI and keeps the cash flow growing. Stock market "corrections" are a dividend investors best friend.

If a stock takes off and goes way up, its yield will probably go way down. I like to hold stocks for as long as possible as I like to keep receiving the distributions they produce. I worked hard to pick that stock and I am not going to give up on it just because its yield is too low. The yield I am receiving is based on the day I bought it, not today. A great blue chip stock will probably be raising its dividends on a regular basis too, which increases my ROI. Let the big boys keep paying you. Let it ride and invest your monthly contributions in a stock with a higher yield. If it goes way down, keep buying. BLUE CHIP STOCKS ONLY!

You are buying low, but NOT selling high, as you are creating wealth for the long term.

Question #3
Exit strategies

MY ORIGINAL PLAN for financial freedom in BYOB was to use a margin account to leverage your growth. It is a powerful strategy, but you will be accumulating debt as you grow your wealth. This is good debt, but debt none the less. When it comes time to transition from growing your wealth to enjoying your new financial freedom lifestyle, you may want to manage your debt by reducing it to a manageable level or eliminating it entirely

If your level of passive income comfortably services your debt while maintaining your lifestyle, then you are good to go. However, if you want to be truly free, debt is a burden that not many people are comfortable living with, so I want to suggest a few ideas to allow you to remove the debt and continue to collect passive income.

I offer three variations. These are, once again, not comprehensive. You are free to combine any of them or come up with your own. I am just priming the pump. If you are at this stage of your investing game, you are probably coming up with all kinds of great ideas all on your own. I would love that.

1. Let the dividends pay down the margin

While you are happily living your life and diligently contributing to YourBank every month, take some time and try to figure out your endgame. By this, I mean try to figure out how much money you will need to earn from passive income so that you are financially free. This could mean you earn enough from your dividends that you can quit working all together, or it could mean that you are free to pursue another type of career that perhaps doesn't pay as much, but is far more fulfilling. The choice is up to you, but make sure you figure out that number so you can design your exit strategy .

As always, I like to recommend that you don't rely on any one source of income to sustain you, as the world can change, and it is best to have a back up plan in case things go sour. Many hands make light work, as they say. So figure out how much you need to make from YourBank in the context of ALL your income streams and write down that number.

Invest faithfully every month until your dividends equal the number you decided upon. At that time, you have several options available to you to ease out of the current "growth" mechanism and onto the "Transition" mechanism. At this point, you have several options.

1. Start living off of your regular pay check again. Take any extra money you have, and only contribute that leftover amount to YourBank. You have two options with your contributions within the portfolio:

- Pay down the margin. This works great as your dividends are paying it down also. Your margin will decrease quickly and you will be able to calculate your freedom date with a pretty good degree of accuracy.
- Or you can continue to buy more stock with your contributions and keep the dividends paying down the margin. The dividends will increase every month, and the margin will eventually be paid off. This method takes a

little longer, but you will enjoy the added
cash-flow

1. Sell some stock. In this case, It probably is best to
   sell the stock that is performing the best from a
   price standpoint, as you can enjoy the added
   benefit of some capital gains. However, this is up
   to you. These stocks have brought you to the
   doorstep of financial freedom. It may be hard to
   part with any of them. This brings you
   backwards from a passive income perspective,
   but allows you to bring your margin ratio back to
   a respectable level. Then you re-adjust to
   method #1.

I PERSONALLY PREFER METHOD #1 as it is a very concise plan.

1. It tells me how much I am going to be making
   every month or quarter
2. I know exactly when my freedom date is
3. It preserves my wealth

I HOPE you understand that these three methods may not be
the only options. The important point is that you have given
yourself options. You have created a choice that few people
ever have to make. Consider yourself one of the privileged

few whose problems are about *what to do with their money*, not how to survive.

As INVESTING IS RISKY AND, frankly, a little scary sometimes, I didn't forget to expand on some ways to protect your assets...

3 WAYS TO PRESERVE YOUR WEALTH

If you have read my book, BYOB, you realize how awesome it is to have an income-producing portfolio of dividend-bearing stocks making you passive income while you sleep. There is no better feeling in the world than realizing you are making money 24 hours a day, without lifting a finger.

THE BIGGEST CONCERN I get about this system is the risk. What will happen if the stock market crashes? How will I preserve my wealth? How do I avoid a margin call?

THESE ARE valid concerns and I spoke very briefly about it in my book. I realize I need to go a little deeper into this topic.

SO HERE ARE THREE ways to mitigate a stock market crash.

Stop

MANY ONLINE BROKERAGES have a feature that is called a STOP. You can initiate a STOP as a sell transaction that has a limit put on it. This is a contingency that you create that tells the brokerage "I want you to sell my stocks when the price is X"

SO HERE YOU would want to determine what your level of comfort is, in the event of a bear market.

You can set any price you wish, and it will depend on your tolerance for fluctuations. In the strategy I offer in my books, where you are "buy and hold" investing, you only really care about the monthly dividends, so a fluctuation means very little to you. Let the stock market crash. You just keep buying as the price falls, and you start to really increase your yield. Sounds pretty good to me.

HOWEVER, if you have ventured into the world of margin accounts and leverage, as explained in the book, then you may have a different opinion about a "correction".

YOU COULD DETERMINE the price that the stock would have to be to trigger a margin call, then set the STOP price at or slightly above that price.

. . .

IE. If you have $1000 of a stock and you have leveraged $500. Then your margin ratio is 50%

If the brokerage allows 70% margin then you would calculate the margin call as follows:

500 / .7 = $714.29 <— This is as low as you can go before a margin call

SO YOU WOULD SET a STOP order at say, $715. If the price falls to that amount it is automatically sold and you are out of the woods.

THE DOWNSIDE of this is you no longer have stocks earning you money. No big deal, you can wait until the price settles, then get back into the market.

THIS IS THE CHEAPEST OPTION, as it is basically free to set a STOP order - but you WILL lose a portion of your equity.

Sell

YOU CAN SELL JUST a portion of your stock in order to change the margin ratio as well. The brokerage will do this automatically if you do not make your margin call payment. The proceeds of the sale will be applied to your outstanding margin balance.

Buy

YOU CAN BUY MORE stock without using leverage - this will lower the margin ratio. Every share that is completely paid for will help reduce the debt ratio.

Pay

YOU CAN PAY off some of the margin amount owing. This will lower the margin percentage. Of course it can be hard to come up with money for these things out of the blue, but if you plan ahead and have a rainy-day fund for this scenario, then you have nothing to worry about.

Options

AS MENTIONED IN THE BOOK, options are a cool way to preserve the total value of your portfolio without losing ANY value.

THINK of options as a type of insurance policy. You are

paying a fee to protect your assets against loss. You would do this for a house or a car, so why not your nest egg?

OPTIONS TRADING CAN BE QUITE complicated and there are as many ways to mix and match in this world as there are lost socks in the laundry hamper. There are many great books written on options trading and you are free to dive down that rabbit hole as you see fit. We will talk about one very particular Options transaction here: the PUT

A PUT OPTION is the right to sell a particular stock at a set price on or before a particular date. You are now in control of when you sell and how much you may sell that stock for. If the stock price crashes, you are laughing, because you have purchased the right to sell it at a price that you agreed upon when you entered into the options contract.

THE GREAT THING about this is that you don't lose ANY of your equity. Your nest egg remains intact. This is a nice feeling. You can sell your stocks at a high price and buy them back later when they are at a discount, therefore increasing your yield and your ROI.

THE ONLY DOWNSIDE to the PUT Options choice is that is can be hard to justify the expense. Options can be expensive as they are based upon the mathematical ratios that are apparent on the day they are bought. There is no discount.

. . .

ONCE AGAIN, if you are getting a nice monthly or quarterly stipend from these stocks, why would you care if the price goes down? You want the dividend income. If that continues, there is no crisis.

REMEMBER: **You only lose money if you sell.**

Set conservation Margin Ratios

LOOK at the history of the stock and see how much it fell in the last stock market crisis (say..2008).

Calculate the price it would likely fall to. Then only leverage to meet the maximum margin ratio at that theoretical price.

EG. If your stock is priced at $100. You could leverage up to $70 at a 70% margin ratio. (This is a common ratio)

If the price fell by 50% (like in the 2008 crash), then 70% of $50 is —> $35.

-If you never borrow more than $35 against that $100 stock, you probably won't run into trouble.

OF COURSE, the stock market is unpredictable and nobody has a crystal ball, so I will put this in **BOLD** type: **STOCK INVESTING INVOLVES RISK.** Please remember that and act accordingly. I am merely suggesting ways to mitigate risk, not remove risk.

. . .

Now, like I mentioned previously, you only lose money on a stock if you actually sell it. If you are not highly leveraged and are happy with the dividend payments you are receiving every month or quarter, then why would you sell a perfectly good stock in a perfectly good company, just because investor sentiment is low at that particular time? Stay in and keep the cash flow machine pumping!

IF YOU HAVE BEEN conservative and stuck to Blue-Chip stocks you will actually celebrate a stock market "correction" as a lower price for great stocks is like getting them on sale! It also gives you a much higher yield on any money you put in at that time, so go crazy. Your passive income machine will be supercharged. When most stock market investors are losing sleep you will be dancing in the streets!

I HIGHLY RECOMMEND reading and learning as much as you can about these strategies as I have just skimmed the surface. Options are a HUGE world, so tread lightly.

BE sure to read my book "BYOB - Be Your Own Bank" to get some REALLY cool ides as to how to invest and grow your wealth.

4

LEVERAGE

The use of leverage to build wealth is a time-honoured tradition that has been the basis for many fortunes. It just makes sense. If you are like me, and most of the people I know, you don't have a ton of money to invest at first. Leverage is a way to increase the SCALE of what you are doing. Increasing the SCALE means all of the components of the deal are proportioned to that scale. As long as the math works, scale is irrelevant.

If you know what you are doing, you evaluate any investment strategy by a few criteria, the most important of which is MATH. If the math works, you usually have a winner. So when you know that you are going to (most likely) get more money OUT of the investment than you put in, and the amounts are always in sync, why not go BIG? If you can get someone to lend you a large sum of money, knowing that the investment will generate enough income to pay back the loan (and hopefully a little more), then you really have to go for it. Leverage is basically using "Other Peoples Money" or OPM to fund your nest egg.

In my book, BYOB, I suggest several ways to maximise

leverage to grow your fortune in ways that you could never do just by using the extra money you have left over at the end of the month. The principles I put forth are powerful and flexible so that you can customise them to suit your lifestyle. I was not so much interested in giving you a "paint-by-numbers" approach as I was trying to demonstrate several possible strategies that can be built using the principles themselves as templates. The principles of leverage, math, cash-flow and time are where the power is.

If you start to gain an understanding of how to use different investment vehicles, math and interest rates, you begin to see you can use these mechanisms to your advantage. There are so many variations that can be put into a practical workflow, that you can set up an automated money system that makes your life easier, while growing your fortune at a rate you never imagined before.

I will take this opportunity to share a couple of "workflows" with you that utilise the power of leverage and math to accelerate your path to financial freedom. I did not invent these methods. I stumbled upon them in my travels. The second method is a variation on an idea I read about in a book entitled "How to Pay off Your Mortgage in Three Years" . Instead of using this method to pay off your mortgage, you can use it to grow your family fortune through dividend investing, like I explain in BYOB.

Remember, leverage is a double-edged sword, It can help you and it can hurt you. Please use leverage responsibly and keep in mind, all investing includes some risk.

Use revolving credit to pay down fixed credit
(Loans, Mortgages)

THIS METHOD INVOLVES A VERY simple mechanism - use simple interest and an open credit vehicle to pay down amortised interest and a closed loan. It might seem simple, yet it is very powerful. It is similar to the old "Smith Manoeuvre" but I feel it is more powerful and slightly more simple.

First, make sure you have a credit card with a healthy credit limit. You are going to be using this credit card for ALL of your monthly expenses, plus any "gotchas" that come along. I think a credit limit that is around 150% of the amount of your desired principle payment would be about right. So if you want to put $10,000 towards your mortgage, make sure you use a credit card that has a $15,000 limit. Of course, you can adjust accordingly to suit your situation. You just want to make sure you are going to be OK in case an unexpected expense pops up - which seems to always be the case.

> *I suggest a credit card that has a rewards program, as you are going to be racking up a ton of points every year. There are many credit cards with flight rewards or cash back. Do some homework and find one that suits your preference. Keep an eye on the fees as they can easily offset any rewards you might accumulate if you are not careful. You are going to be building a fortune quickly, why not get a free vacation while you are at it?*

So we will assume you are starting with a $0 balance on your card, but it can still work if you have a little owing, you just need to make sure you have enough to cover your expenses.

If you have an open mortgage, you should be able to contribute large lump sums towards the principle at any time. Some mortgages have rules around this activity, such as you can only put down 10% of the original balance in any given year. This makes the system a little harder to maximise, but it still will accelerate your pay down dramatically.

The first thing you do is put $10,000 directly from your CC into your mortgage. This will reduce the principle by 10K. This also leaves you $5000 available credit in case of emergencies. Make sure the 10K goes towards your principle when you make extra payments. You don't want this lump sum going towards interest.

Then, when you get paid, you put your ENTIRE paycheque onto the credit card. This reduces your balance owing by the full amount of your monthly paycheck. This reduces your interest payment as your average daily balance is less than the 10K. Then, throughout the month you run it back up again as you spend to live your life.

Here is the key: SPEND LESS THAN YOU EARN. I cannot emphasise this enough. There is no magic money strategy in the world that will allow you to overspend and still get ahead. It is mathematically impossible. So just don't do it.

Each month, as you keep paying down your credit card with your paycheque, you are running up the total by the difference in your earnings and your spending.

For example, if you put your entire pay check , 100% on the credit card, but only spend 80% per month, you will reduce the balance owing by a full 20% of your income every month. Eventually, you will have paid the entire credit card off.

Then you take another 10K and put it on your mortgage.

Rinse and repeat.

Do this over and over again until your mortgage is paid off, saving you potentially thousands of dollars in interest over the lifetime of the mortgage. This will also take years off of the mortgage term. You can celebrate by taking a vacation with all of the reward points you have earned!

A Slightly More Sophisticated Method

THIS METHOD INVOLVES USING a Line of Credit (LOC), a Credit Card (CC) , and a mortgage.

The LOC can be a Home Equity Line of Credit HELOC or a personal LOC. It is up to you. This method has a little bit more flexibility built into it as you now have TWO buffers against crazy things happening.

First, let's assume you have a $50,000 LOC.

You take the $50,000 and put it on your mortgage, paying down only the principal. Then every month you put your entire paycheque into the LOC. This will reduce the amount owing by the full amount of your paycheck. Then you live entirely off of your Credit Card for the month. At the end of the month, you borrow from your LOC to pay off your CC in its entirety. This way you pay no interest on the CC! This also allows you to only pay the interest on the original 50K minus the amount of your paycheque.

Each month you pay down the LOC by **spending less than you earn**. Over time, the LOC balance becomes 0 and you take another 50K and pay down your mortgage again. This timeframe will only be as fast as you are willing to commit to spending less than you earn each month. If you are not thrifty, it will take a long time.

The interesting little benefits of this plan are:

a. You are continuing to make mortgage payments at the original agreed upon rate with your mortgage lender. Since you paid down the principle owing, each monthly mortgage payment you make pays off MORE principal and LESS interest than it normally would have if you had not paid the 50K towards the principle.

b. The interest on the LOC and the CC are calculated in the following way. It is called Daily average balance or Daily average balance owing. They take the amount owing each day, and multiply it by the yearly interest rate divided by 365. Then at the end of the month they add them all up and that is what you pay. If you reduce the average daily amount owing by the amount of your paycheque, you will have saved yourself interest as you did not borrow that month's expenses until the END of the month to pay down your CC. You kept the balance as low as you could for the whole month. Then you pay off your CC at the end of the month and are immediately putting in your next months paycheque.

c. Most CCs do not charge you ANY interest if you pay the balance off completely before the due date. So by paying the entire balance off every month with the LOC you are not paying the CC interest.

Use the Money to Grow

If you have read my book, BYOB - Be Your Own Bank, you may have incorporated my plan to invest ALL of your pay check into your family fortune. If that is the case, cool. That method is the best way I know to maximise your investment contribution. However, some of you may feel that there is too much risk involved in that method, and that is OK. You have to feel comfortable while doing this stuff, or else you will lose sleep at night and nobody wants that. These ideas are supposed to improve and enhance our quality of life, not make it worse. So don't worry.

There is a less risky, almost as effective, way to grow your wealth.

Instead of using the CC or LOC to make a lump sum payment on a loan, you can make a lump sum contribution to your family fortune. This will instantly create cash flow and give you margin room for whatever you would like to use it for. This is nice, as when first getting YourBank going it can feel like it is taking FOREVER to get any substantial dividends. Now you can get some pretty nice distributions right away and re-invest them or use them to help pay down the CC or LOC and accelerate the plan! Leverage is awesome.

Once you have paid down the LOC to zero, you can do it all over again. You are not limited to the restrictions that a mortgage might have, you can go crazy. Every time you put the lump sum into the portfolio, your dividends go up, and your cash flow increases. If you are using the cash flow from the dividends to help pay down the LOC, you will be accelerating the pay down rate, and you can reinvest quicker each and every time!

You will be able to experience the real results of leverage and compounding that the rich enjoy. Once those dividends are coming in every month, you will feel powerful and lighter. Your financial burdens will no longer be carried by you trading your time for a pay check. Your money will be helping to carry the load.

Debt interest curve vs. investment interest curve

WHEN YOU FIRST CALCULATE THE return on investment and the interest costs, they may not look good at first. The interest cost may be more than the returns and it will appear to be a bad investment; however, if you realize that these things change over time, then it starts to make sense when you factor in the curves and absolute amounts.

Absolute Amounts

IF YOU CALCULATE the interest on the $10,000 LOC over 3 years and the dividends on the investment over the same time period they work out to:

ASSUME 4.5% INTEREST
    Assume 5% Yield
    Assume $2000 per month pay-down (you spend $2000 less than you earn)

With a $2000 DIFFERENCE MONTHLY

Date	Amount Owning	Interest	Portfolio Balance	Dividends
January	$10000.00	$375.00	$10000.00	$416.67
February	$8000.00	$300.00	$10000.00	$416.67
March	$6000.00	$225.00	$10000.00	$416.67
April	$4000.00	$150.00	$10000.00	$416.67
May	$2000.00	$75.00	$10000.00	$416.67
June	$0.00	$0.00	$10000.00	$416.67
July	$10000.00	$375.00	$20000.00	$833.33
August	$8000.00	$300.00	$20000.00	$833.33
September	$6000.00	$225.00	$20000.00	$833.33
October	$4000.00	$150.00	$20000.00	$833.33
November	$2000.00	$75.00	$20000.00	$833.33
December	$0.00	$0.00	$20000.00	$833.33
January	$10000.00	$375.00	$30000.00	$1250.00
February	$8000.00	$300.00	$30000.00	$1250.00
March	$6000.00	$225.00	$30000.00	$1250.00
April	$4000.00	$150.00	$30000.00	$1250.00
May	$2000.00	$75.00	$30000.00	$1250.00
June	$0.00	$0.00	$30000.00	$1250.00
July	$10000.00	$375.00	$40000.00	$1666.67
August	$8000.00	$300.00	$40000.00	$1666.67
September	$6000.00	$225.00	$40000.00	$1666.67
October	$4000.00	$150.00	$40000.00	$1666.67
November	$2000.00	$75.00	$40000.00	$1666.67
December	$0.00	$0.00	$40000.00	$1666.67
Total		$4500.00		$25000.00

1

In this scenario, you paid $4500 interest, but earned $25000 in dividends. That is a difference of $21500! What you do with the extra money is up to you. If you make a similar spreadsheet with your own interest rates and income amounts, you will see that same results.

If you use the dividends to pay down the principle on the LOC, along with your regular payments, you will accelerate the plan exponentially.

. . .

THIS CHART SHOWS A VERY simple and, perhaps extreme, example of what I am talking about, but the point is to demonstrate that you should always look at the total amount of interest and returns you make over the life of the investment to see if it is worthwhile. You shouldn't be fooled by a slightly higher interest rate on your LOC, or Credit card, as you will have a plan to pay it back over a very short period of time.

I make a huge number of spreadsheets for any of my ideas, and plug in a ton of different numbers and scenarios in order to make a plan that works for my life. If you have the math in front of you, you can make much better decisions about your investment strategy and see how long it will take to accomplish any particular plan. If you build it correctly, can play with the numbers to accelerate your timelines, or maximise your returns. Take emotion out of the equation and let the numbers do the decision making.

Welcome to investing like the rich!

5

PHILOSOPHY

Why build up a giant nest-egg only to spend it? Why not build it up and keep it?

The traditional way most people are taught to manage their money and save for the future usually follows something similar to this:

1. Go to school
2. Do as you are told
3. Be a good student
4. Do your homework
5. Get good grades
6. Don't buck the system
7. Go to College
8. Do as you are told
9. Be a good student
10. Do your homework
11. Get good grades
12. Don't buck the system
13. Run up thousands of dollars in student loans

(You are now beholden to someone who stands to profit from your debt)

14. Get a good Job
15. Do as you are told
16. Be a good employee
17. Do your work
18. Get good annual reviews
19. Don't buck the system
20. Contribute to an RRSP or 401K plan (You are now giving control of your hard-earned cash to someone else who stand to profit from your savings.)
21. Repeat for 40 years
22. Retire - Retirement usually is the result of:

a. Being too old to work
b. Finally having enough saved up to live off of
c. Being eligible for Old age pensions and social security
d. Dying

24. Convert your RRSP or 401K into a LIF or RIF (You are again giving control of your hard earned cash to someone else who stands to profit from your savings.)
25. Spend your money until it is gone or you die.

So your wealth curve looks similar to this:

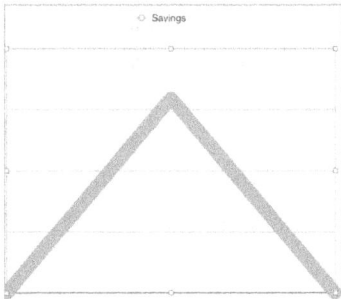

THE PEAK of this chart is your retirement date. So this method really consists of: Save up your money, then spend it all. Then hope that you don't run out of money before you die. To make matters worse, the whole time you are saving and spending it, the money is in the hands of someone who is taking out 1-3% every year in the form of "fees" in order to "manage" your portfolio for you - because it is assumed that you are an idiot and can't take care of your own money.

Perhaps I can suggest to you that there is another way to approach this. In my book BYOB, I suggest that you could save up your money, and then keep it. Why get rid of it as soon as you get it? You do this through dividend investing. You do this through creating passive income. You do this through creating multiple streams of income. As your nest egg grows, your passive income grows. You then live off of the income your nest-egg produces forever. Not only do you NEVER run out of money, but your heirs will inherit this machine. Your family fortune will continue to remain intact as long as those remaining in the family trust don't do something foolish with it...

I believe that in order to truly experience financial freedom, and the spoils of wealth, you need to *have* money. I like to think that not having to worry about where your next dollar is coming from is the goal. If you have a nest-egg and you worry about whether it is going to outlive you or not, then you are not truly free. If you only worry about whether your heirs are going to squander it after you are gone, that is an entirely different thing.

The philosophy of financial freedom is based on a simple principle:

Invest your money in income producing assets so that you don't have to work for your money anymore, your money works for you.

Now this is great. Assets can be stocks, GICs, a business, bank interest or many other vehicles.

Passive income can be dividends, interest, profit from a business, or many other things as well.

Of course the key mathematical foundation of this idea is that you spend less than you earn. All the other mechanisms are built upon this foundation. This is why I emphasise and repeat this several times in this book, and the last. There is no other idea more critical to your success than this one.

It occurred to me the other day, while I was engaging in the age old argument with someone of "whether to invest or pay down debt" that financial freedom begs the same question. Since financial freedom is the result of earning more passive income than your expenses, why not lessen the burden on your assets and reduce your expenses.

This simple idea strikes me as rather profound. It has so many implications, yet seems too obvious to be contemplated deeply.

I will offer a few thoughts on how amazing this simple idea could be:

1. When you earn more income, you are obligated to pay income tax on it. Therefore, if you need an extra $1000 a month to meet your expenses, you will need to earn *in excess of* $1000 to take home the required amount. Depending on your tax bracket, this could be up to DOUBLE that amount. Yikes!

2. If you reduce your expenses by $1000, the amount you are ahead is exactly $1000. No income taxes involved.

3. Building a wealth creation machine is hard work and can take a long time. The point of building this machine is to be financially free. If your expenses are minimal, then it is a lot easier and will take a lot less time to get there. If you have embarked on your wealth creation journey you will understand what I mean. Financial freedom is a destination and a journey.

HAVING ACHIEVED a state in your life where your passive income has exceeded your expenses, you are now free. This is not where you stop. This is where you begin your new adventure where you no longer need to trade your time for money. You are the master of your life.

Once you are free from employment slavery, you can keep growing!

DON'T BE A VICTIM - TAKE CONTROL OF
YOUR FINANCIAL FUTURE

A s I mentioned briefly before, it makes no sense to give your hard earned money over to someone else to "manage" for you. If you are reading this book, I assume that you may have an interest in taking MORE responsibility for your personal wealth, not less. That is great. Here is my pitch to you.

Mutual funds were designed to be a miniature "index fund" in that they take a whole bunch of stocks and group them together under one roof and sell portions of the group to investors. You own a tiny piece of the whole group, and the mutual find managers take a small fee for creating and managing this fund. This is great if you are a hands-off type of investor and really don't care about this kind of stuff.

The problem here is that, no matter whether this investment makes money or not, the mutual fund manager makes money. They take their 3% fee every year, like clockwork, no matter whether they did a good job or not of growing your fortune. I can't really believe there is much incentive for them to try really hard at growing the value of the mutual fund other than they might really be nice people and want the best for their customers. I think their shareholders may be a slightly higher priority...

Tony Robbins does a great job of explaining the pitfalls and issues with this approach in his books "Money - Master the Game" and "Unshakable". I highly recommend them.

MONEY:MASTER the Game - Amazon.com
Unshakable - Amazon.com

MY APPROACH INVOLVES you taking complete control of your wealth, and keeping control of it.

Yes, you are still investing in companies that you personally do not control, however, you are eliminating the middle man. You are buying stocks in blue-chip companies that you hand-picked yourself, and are being paid out directly from the companies themselves, in the form of dividends.

By growing your portfolio yourself, and by keeping your portfolio, you are taking control and keeping control over your financial future. You worked really hard for that money, so you deserve to keep it. It has been said many times, "It is not how much money you earn, it is how much money you KEEP". Truer words were never spoken, my friend. When you hear rich people talk about their relative financial status with each other, they don't usually speak in terms of "I earn this much per year". They speak in terms of "This is my net-worth".

Net-worth is the true measure of wealth. This is how you gauge your financial clout in the world. This is your leverage to create more wealth. A high net-worth allows you to:

1. Earn passive income from your money working

2. Use your net-worth for leverage - Such as borrowing from the banks to invest.
3. Create a safety-net in case of disaster
4. Contribute to charity. You can make a true difference in the world when you are wealthy.
5. If you really had to, you could actually spend your nest-egg.

ONE OF THE really cool ideas I explore is the fact that you can continue to grow your nest-egg for your entire life! Why would you stop caring about money or how it works once you retire. What is "retirement" anyway? I define it as financial freedom. It just means I don't have to have a traditional job. I don't have to trade my time for money anymore. I don't have to do something I don't want to do or HATE to do in order to earn a living. I am retired when I make decisions about how I spend my time based on what I feel like doing. I spend my time exactly as I see fit. I don't have a boss. I am the boss (don't tell my wife).

I love investing. I love to formulate money strategies. I love to write books about my ideas. I love to help people learn about money and investing. I love to share my ideas with as many people as possible. Why would I stop doing that? Does being old mean not doing anything anymore? Not on my watch..

So it goes for your family fortune. Why would you stop growing it just because you are 65? I suggest you ALWAYS live on less than you earn and invest the difference. If you are financially free, that means you can live the life you want on your passive income, and still have some left over that you continue to invest in your passive income machine.

You need to always be growing as a person or you are dying. I believe that same holds true for your fortune. It must always be growing or it is dying. There is no "set it and forget it". This almost guarantees that it will whither and die. Life is designed for growth. Nothing ever just stays static. You must grow and nurture your family fortune and it will always take care of you. Of course, you must teach these principles to your heirs if they want to continue to live off of the spoils of your hard work.

Once you understand how powerful and freeing it is to have a family fortune, I hope you will be able to see just how weird it seems to consider spending it all until you run out of money or die. Most people will always choose to keep growing their wealth, as inflation will always continue, and your family will probably keep expanding.

You are free to spend it all. You can do that if you hate your heirs and you are determined not to leave it to anyone. Then go crazy. I'm not here to tell you how to live your life. I just want to suggest to you that the alternative is an option. I feel my obligation to you is to let you know that you can build up a fortune and then KEEP IT.

It has been suggested by those in psychological circles that one measure of mental health is the extent to which we take responsibility for our circumstances. We have what is called a "locus of control" mechanism in our brain that determines how we perceive our lives and how much we believe we are in control of our circumstances.

If we believe that our station in life is the result of outside influences then we are taking a victim stance. We believe that "things that are out of our control" have made our lives one way or another. This is considered an unhealthy way to approach life and it can lead to poor decisions and sometimes frustration and despair.

The "proactive" approach or empowerment viewpoint suggests that we take responsibility for EVERYTHING that happens in our lives. No matter what circumstances befall us, we choose to believe that we are responsible . This leads us to choose our responses to outside influence instead of feeling victimised. This leads us to be focused on actions. This leads us to begin thinking creatively and finding ways to improve our situation. This is a healthy attitude, by all accounts.

I am encouraging you to take the same approach when it comes to your financial situation.

So much traditional financial advice lures you into being a victim. It does this by persuading you to give over your power to an "expert". It does this by suggesting you "buy low, sell high". It does this by leading you to the slaughter in the form of "be a good student and a good employee and we will reward you for your compliance".

If you are reading this book and understanding it (it is not hard), I assume you have the intelligence to manage your own money. It is not scary. It is not complicated. I encourage you to take the proactive approach and own your results.

There is no lack of financial information out there. My message to you is, learn as much as you can so you can make informed decisions about your money.

The old Japanese proverb goes something like this:

"Getting money is like digging with a needle. Spending it is like water soaking into the sand."

7

WIN AT THE GAME OF MONEY

I was born into a middle class family in a small town in Canada. Neither of my parents had a college degree. My Dad left school in grade eight. They had good jobs, and provided a nice comfortable life for us. We didn't enjoy many luxuries, but we never went without. They were shining examples of what was possible if you "worked hard, saved your money, and were a good person".

My parents encouraged us to work for our own money, not just ask for it. I appreciate that they did that as I realized early that you cannot get something for nothing. This was a valuable lesson that applies in the real world, and that I find some people still haven't figured out yet. Look at how many people play the lottery. This is a classic example of wanting something for nothing.

The lesson that taught us was great, but that was about the best they could do. Any information about how the world actually worked, and especially about investing, capitalism, entrepreneurship, or wealth creation was completely beyond their understanding. They came from a world where they could have a nice, comfortable life without that knowledge.

My dad retired at 55 years old with a fantastic pension and my mom soon followed. They never had to learn about money, other than making it last for a full month, because they didn't have to. They came from a long bygone era, where there was a chicken in every pot and a chevy in every driveway.

I have some bad news for you. Those days are gone.

Inflation rates are out of control.

Pensions are very rare

Job security is an antiquated concept.

Competition is everywhere. Competition for jobs, competition for business, competition for customers, and competition for acceptance into the best schools.

The capitalist system we live in has not really changed for centuries. It continues to benefit those that understand it, and punish those that don't. It has always been that way, yet it is even more intense today because of the disappearing middle class. My parents' lifestyle is harder and harder to attain today because of the system and its rules.

Capitalism is just a series of rules that everyone has agreed upon. It is a system of exchange of something of value for something else of value. Not hard to figure out, but extremely hard to keep in perspective. We, as a human race, seem to always take things to the nth degree until it implodes upon itself - and capitalism is no exception. What started out as a system of barter, has become a system that has no bounds. It has become the basis of our entire society, a foundation upon which we all rest, yet we do not realize it.

We are born into a capitalist world, where those that know the rules of the game win and those that don't, struggle. It doesn't seem fair that we are forced to play, even if we were not told the rules. The game is rigged.

Inflation

I read an <u>article</u> recently that completely turned inflation on its head. It made the point that the "published" inflation rate or index is an average of a large list of products and services, some of which have a greater or lesser bearing on your life. It includes everything from pens to hockey sticks. However, if you look specifically at things that are vital to our existence or are of major impact on our lives, the situation gets a little scary. Things like housing, rent, higher education and even food have dramatically outpaced the standard inflation rate.

STATS FROM THE ARTICLE:

IE. in the year **1950**
    The average Family income: **$3,300** ($275 monthly)
    The average Car: **$1,510**
    The median Home Price: **$7,354**

So LET'S look at these numbers as a percentage of annual income:

CAR: 1,510 ÷ 3300 = **45.7%** or about 5 1/2 months income
    House: 7354 ÷ 3300 = 2.23 or **2.2 years** of income (26.75 months income)

. . .

COMPARE to **2014**
    The average Family Income:**$51,017** ($4,251 Monthly)
    The average Car:$31,252
    The Median Home Price:$188,900

NOW LET'S look at today's numbers as a percentage of income:

CAR:31,252/51,017 = **61%** or about 7.35 months income
    House:188,900/51,017 - 3.7 or **3.7 years** of income (44.43 months income)

IF I SHOWED you the statistics on Medical costs or post secondary education you would be appalled. Even since 2001 inflation rates for these items has been a whopping 145%.

UNIVERSITY OF CALIFORNIA AT DAVIS:
    2004 in-state tuition $5,684
    2015 in state tuition $13,951

THERE IS a LONG list of colleges that have DOUBLED their tuition in the ten years from 2004 to 2014. I am not sure they are going to slow down any time soon.

. . .

THIS ARTICLE (US based data) freaked me out a little so I looked up the stats for my hometown:

2002

    Median Family Income: $61,200
    2016
    Median Family Income: $89,610

INCOMES WENT UP **46.42%**

COST INCREASE (%) since 2002

ALL ITEMS : 35%
    Food: 41.5%
    Housing: **62.5%**
    Gasoline: 36%
    Transportation: 30.5%

THESE STATS ARE UP to 2016. If you look up to 2018 they get even worse (Gas: 83.1% increase since 2002). The BIG things in life that we tend to need like food and shelter are going up faster than our salaries. Higher education is costing more. I don't even know how to calculate health care costs for those of you who live in the US. (I live in Canada - we have universal health care. Nice)

    I am not trying to be negative here, I just want to try to emphasise that the world of capitalism isn't about to take a break, or let you off the hook. You need to participate in the system so you might as well jump in with your eyes wide open.

What can we do about it?

Educate **Ourselves**

OUR FIRST RESOURCE TO help us to learn the rules is our parents. If our folks know what they are doing, hopefully they teach us about money and how it works so we are equipped to go out into the world armed with the information we need to succeed.

Unfortunately, most parents don't know the rules. They are like my folks, who just have a basic model to follow, and it worked great for them in a different time. It no longer is very useful.

To say that the system is unfair, would be an understatement. As the world is completely and utterly driven by commerce, for good and bad, you would think that it would be a prerequisite to know how money works. But it isn't. Maybe it isn't in the best interest of those who do understand the game to have that information become common knowledge. I don't know.

Basic financial education should be taught in school . This has been said by many who understand the inner workings of the system, and it should be continued. We must arm our children with the tools they need to succeed in the world. If we are all going to agree to base all of human existence on capitalism, then maybe we should all agree to learn about it. It just seems like the logical thing to do, right?

So, since money is not talked about in school, young people are blindly following the standard paradigm and going to school, getting good grades and getting a good job, etc.

You have to realize that there are those people and institutions in the world that stand to profit from this whole system. This is not a system designed to maximise your life, it is designed to maximise theirs. You have been led to the slaughter.

The good news is, there is something you can do about it. You can educate yourself.

I started out knowing NOTHING about money, finance or wealth creation. I didn't even realize I didn't know. I was completely oblivious to the information I really needed. But as circumstances presented themselves, out of necessity, I had to learn. I learned one thing at a time as I needed to. One nugget of info, that might help me through that particular financial challenge I was having, and I was able to move forward. Each time my life became a financial crisis I was forced to learn more.

As I really HATE struggling financially, I was determined to figure out how to get myself off of the treadmill.

A bit of wisdom I came across a long time ago really made me think. It went something like this: "If you want to change the world, start with yourself". I think that might be an amalgamation of many sayings I have heard, but in this instance, it really applies. We are not about to change the world so that financial education is freely available to all. It may be the end goal, but in the meantime, we can educate ourselves, and maybe pass that information on to our children. After all, we are all playing the game, whether we want to or not. Instead of changing the game, let's learn to play it. If you can't beat 'em, join 'em.

The key concept that I am trying to get across to you is that the information is actually out there for you to educate yourself. There are hundreds, if not thousands, of books about money, investing, finance, and leverage. Some are better than others, but the truth is, this information is not a secret, it is just up to you to actively seek it out. The hardest part of all this is convincing people that they DON'T know what they are doing and that they NEED to educate themselves. They don't realize that they would be much more effective in the world if they had all the information than if they are just told to do what everyone else is doing. The point of education sometimes is not the information you learn, but its ability to promote critical thinking. When you create new synapses in your brain, it doesn't happen in a vacuum. Everything is attached to everything else. A new insight about money and finance may help you to negotiate a raise at work, or come up with a better plan for managing your time. The human brain is an amazing thing, and feeding it new information is the key to happiness. Modern psychology has determined that the primary issue with anxiety and depression is rumination, or repetitive thinking. When you create new synapses in your brain, you interrupt the old patterns and allow new thoughts and ideas to enter your consciousness. This keeps us interested and engaged in the world around us and gets us "out of our heads". This allows us to see the world from new perspectives and we can get out of old patterns and non-beneficial habits a little bit easier.

So by reading a book that teaches you something, or taking a class, or attending a seminar, or watching a video about something and applying what you learned, you are taking a huge step towards self realisation. This is the peak of Maslow's hierarchy of needs and there is no higher pursuit for a person.

Keep interested and curious.

The most valuable resource we have, is time. It is precious beyond measure. We all have been given the same amount of time in any given day. And we know that we will all eventually run out of time. This is inevitable. So valuing our time is one of the most self respecting things we can do. So we need to evaluate our "time spending" as much as our "money spending". We need to think about how much time we put into certain activities. Such as:

Surviving - We live in a world where if we don't earn money we will die. Everything costs money. So it is incumbent upon us to get money from somewhere to pay to live. We need food, clothing and shelter. Until they roll out Universal Basic Income everywhere, this is just a fact of life. So depending on our earning ability, there is a certain percentage of our time that needs to be spent on making sure we have food, clothing and shelter. Even cavemen had to spend their time on these things. It is not a capitalist thing, it is a life on earth thing.

Self Improvement - We can only increase our earning ability and decrease the amount of time we spend on surviving if we improve ourselves. We live in a knowledge based economy now. Those who know how, do well. Those who don't know how, are left behind. The best investment you can make is to invest in yourself. Learn as much as you can. Then you can take back some time for the really important things in life.

Creating - This is a broad category, but I like to think that there are two types of activities in our world, creation and consumption. You are either being a creator, and bringing forth value into the world, or you are being a consumer by using or consuming valuables. We are all a creator or a consumer every day, but which do you spend the most time on? I suggest the most valuable use of your time would be to spend it as a creator, as that usually can translate into income. Consuming usually results in money leaving your hands and going to some other person who created something. We all need to consume, but it is important to realize that creation is what drives the world. Capitalism is fuelled by creation.

Money has to flow. The economy is healthy when money is being spent. It is based on growth, but money is just a symbol. What REALLY needs to grow is value. We need to keep creating more VALUE in the world and money will flow around and through it and help keep the system healthy. If we hoard money, or try to get something for nothing, or have a win/lose mentality, that will kill the economy. There has to actually be value exchanged. Money will never sustain the economy, only value will. People who think that they are "shrewd" by taking advantage of other people and not returning equal value are just hurting themselves in the end, as that type of thinking is what destroys economies. We need to offer fair value in exchange for money. We all prosper when there is a symbiotic relationship between value and money. Value for value is the only sustainable system. Greed and corruption are the harbingers of a sick economy, and can never keep it afloat. The very system they are trying to exploit will collapse because of that attitude. Money needs to flow. Just like a living organism, stagnation will cause sickness and death.

By arming yourself with knowledge about money, finance and how the game of capitalism is played you are giving yourself a better chance to succeed in this world. You never know which nugget of information you come across in a book, seminar or course will be the difference maker in your life. It sometimes takes just one idea to change the world.

MULTIPLE STREAMS OF INCOME

E ach transaction or machine cog doesn't have to be a home run. We tend to think this way because we were trained to do only one thing at a time.

We were a student.

Then we were a College student.

Then we were an employee at ONE company and we had ONE job title at a time with usually a focus on ONE objective.

If you look at successful people in many walks of life, they tend to have accumulated success over time via multiple contributions to their field. It is very rare for a person whom we might consider successful to have only ever done ONE thing. That seems silly, now that we have said it out loud. It is usually the culmination of multiple efforts that creates success. I learned this when I was a musician and songwriter.

As is typical of most artists, when you write your first song, or paint your first painting, or write your first book, your are completely infatuated with it. It is your baby. You put so much love and attention into it, and it was hard to do because you had never done it before. You feel it is a part of you and the ultimate expression of who you are and what you are about. You are intimately familiar with every intricate detail of it, and you have a naive hope that everyone in the world will see it the way that you do.

Then you write another song... and then another.

Eventually you write a hundred songs. The next morning, you wake up after writing that hundredth song and you realize that not every song you wrote is a gem. You realize that some songs are better than others. You reluctantly admit that maybe some of them are not so wonderful. You now have perspective.

This same sort of perspective applies to most producers of anything, There are consumers, and there are producers. Producers create things and present them to the world. Consumers see all that is produced, and take them in. Hopefully as producer, you can make lots of consumers like what you have produced and have them give you money for it. That is the dream.

When you look at people whom we might call successful "producers", they tend to have a body of work that defines their success, not just one piece of work. Most successful entrepreneurs have failed at a few businesses before they found one that worked. Most artists created many, many pieces of work before they had an impact. Most writers that are considered successful have several books. This approach to defining and creating success is the time-honoured template for most people. One-hit wonders are few and far between. This same philosophy should apply to your portfolio and your passive income plan.

You should research and evaluate many stocks, and then pick a few. Then do it again and again. Eventually you will find a good 10 to 12 that really make sense. Each one will produce passive income at its own pace. This is the only sensible way to create your machine. Add them all together for a robust and workable plan. Never rely on one stock or one machine to do it all.

In that same vein, you also need to look at your whole income portfolio, not just the dividend-bearing stocks in your margin account. Look at multiple streams of income. Dividends are wonderful. I LOVE THEM - but I would be foolish to rely on just the stock market to take care of me. I have pursued other methods of creating income that will be a part of my overall strategy to "Live off of money that I didn't trade my time for". Many hands makes light work.

In addition to building my passive income machine via dividend-bearing securities, I also write books, create online training courses, and have invested in a few business. I also currently have a full time career as a telecommunications executive.

I hope to be making enough from my passive income streams to retire if I wish to, but I actually really enjoy my full time job and will continue to work there until I want to move on. The key here is that I really want the CHOICE to continue working or not. Having the choice to do as you please because money is no longer an issue is true free-dom. Financial Freedom is sometimes mistaken for "relax-ing" or "retiring" but it is actually just a state of being. It is a mind-set. When you have enough money so that you don't have to spend your time trying to survive, then you are free.

You must understand. Nothing in this world is a certainty. We owe it to ourselves, if we are to take full responsibility for our lives, to prepare for all inevitabilities. Any one source of income could suddenly become unavail-able or erratic. This is just how things are. We are choosing not to be victims so we take control of the possible outcomes.

Multiple streams of income is a smart idea for everyone. This is not just for the rich, or those people who have built a cool money machine. This is for everyone who knows that they can depend on themselves to guarantee their future. This is for the ordinary guy who has just a 9-5 job.

I like to consider myself a jack of all trades type of guy who really isn't the master of anything. I have many interests and I am passionate about a few. The beauty of having several streams of income is that none of them have to be amazing. You don't have to corner the market in any one discipline to reap the rewards. If you do ok in several areas, the cumulative output of the whole creates a nice body of work and hopefully an adequate level of passive income.

My books don't have to be all #1 bestsellers. I just need to try my hardest to create the best quality content I know how to. Then I need to do it over and over again. I just need to keep creating. Every creation will hopefully appeal to, and be able to help, someone. Then, if enough people resonate with my work, I can make a little money from that pursuit. If I add up my body of work over time, I hope to earn a decent living.

Multiple streams of income, as a concept, has been around a long time. I remember reading about it in the 90's, and it probably existed long before that. The idea is very prevalent in real estate, as that is one of the most popular secondary income streams there is.

Real estate is a great way to invest, and it is accessible to almost everyone, if you have the right information. There are many great books and courses out there that teach you how to invest in real estate - even with "no money down", as they say. I gave real estate a bad wrap in BYOB, however it is still a great way to grow your wealth, and make some passive income if you do it properly.

I am encouraging you to think outside the box. I want you to see the possibilities that understanding these concepts will give you. By understanding my system, and pursuing as many income opportunities as you are able, you can truly get to understand and experience what it is like to taste true freedom.

AFTERWORD

A NEW WORLD

I hope that you found the ideas I have presented informative and helpful. I tried to make the information as clear as possible without droning on and on. Many people commented that they loved how short my last book was, as personal finance is kind of a dry topic, and they appreciated how I got right to the point.

I know I am a big fan of, "Don't bore us, get to the chorus", yet, in doing so, sometimes the necessary "boring" details are missing.

I hope that I was able to fill in some blanks without being boring. I love learning about this kind of thing myself and I have read hundreds of books on the subjects of investing, personal finance and financial freedom. I like to assume that my readers are of the same ilk. I am speaking to you as a colleague and friend, whom I would want to see grow into a seasoned investor who is achieving his or her dreams of financial freedom. I apologize if I made any assumptions in my writing about what you might already know or don't know.

I love to learn, so I continue to read and attend seminars

to further my financial education. I encourage you to do the same. When you are empowered with new ideas and information, a whole new world opens up. A new world of possibilities where you might find hope where there was none before. This new world can be a bit scary, but it is also exciting. You will benefit from the positive changes that this new information brings both to your finances, and your mind. You are becoming more.

I hope to continue to provide ideas and strategies to you as I learn more and gain wisdom from my own financial adventures.

If you are interested in joining me on this journey you can keep in touch through the following:

The BYOB Website:
    https://www.beyourownbank.ca

My Personal Website:
    https://periscott.com

Thanks

ABOUT THE AUTHOR

Peri Scott is a regular guy who has spent 30 years perfecting his financial strategy. He lives with his family in Canada.

This is Peri's second book.

www.beyourownbank.ca

www.periscott.com

ALSO BY PERI SCOTT

BYOB - Be Your Own Bank